Hearing Voices

Volume 5: Collected Stories & Drawings of Brian Andreas

StoryPeople
Decorah

ISBN 0-9642660-5-9

The people in this book, if at one time real, are now entirely fictitious, having been subjected to a combination of a selective memory and a fertile imagination. Any resemblance to real people you might know, even if they are the author's relatives, is entirely coincidental, and is a reminder that you are imagining the incidents in this book as much as the author is.

StoryPeople
P.O. Box 64
Decorah, IA 52101
USA
319.382.8060
319.382.0263 FAX

storypeople@storypeople.com
http://www.storypeople.com/

First edition: July, 1998

Printed at the West Coast Print Center, Berkeley, California

To my sons, David Quinn & Matthew Shea, for all their exuberance & questions & completely original way of simplifying complicated things

& always, to Ellen, my partner & love, for her life & passion & song & for reminding me of the dreams you must never leave behind...

Other books by Brian Andreas available
from StoryPeople Press:

Mostly True
Still Mostly True
Going Somewhere Soon
Strange Dreams
Story People

Cover Art: Brian Andreas
Back photo: Jon Duder

Hearing Voices

Introduction

I've been hearing voices for a long time now. Not great choirs of angelic voices that come down in a blaze of glory. Not the voices of the prophets, or the news at eleven, or the jumble of psychic static that comes with too many people in one place. The voices I hear are soft voices, filled with sunlight & the warmth of the earth, letting me know that everything I touch & see & feel is alive. They want me to know that they're doing well, in case I'm interested.

For a long while, I thought I was special, that I had been chosen to make sense of everything they told me. If I could put the voices together, perhaps find their hidden pattern, the quick connections between them, I'd have the secret of life. I'd be like the alchemists of old, armed with the Philosopher's Stone, able to make the dead dance & the living soar, turn water into wine, rocks into gold. I'd have power beyond my wildest dreams.

Fortunately, the voices had other ideas. They reminded me that I didn't know as much as I pretended to. They told me to act now, but they didn't leave an operator standing by. They made me laugh out loud when everybody else was being serious. They argued in public & made me wait until they finished. They didn't stop to ask for directions. They never believed that sometimes I needed sleep, so they stayed up late & talked back to the tv. They spoke through anybody who happened to be nearby, not really caring whether I wanted to listen or not. They were good at saying, I told you so, but they tried not to. They liked the smell of wet dirt after a rain & weeding the garden & the way a baby's head wobbles when it first sits up & they weren't afraid to admit it. They yelled at me when I did stupid things, but they usually sat down & helped me figure out a way to fix it. They liked to pretend that they were scared of the dark, but I wasn't fooled. They whispered in my ear constantly, telling me to notice this, watch that, don't forget.

Finally, I learned to just listen, & unexpectedly, they taught me the secret of life. Be a lover. That was it: be a lover. When you love, whether a child, or your work, or the feel of the wind licking your skin, you are in a state of grace. You aren't asking your love to be anything more than what it is. The paradox is that what it is, is beyond imagining. It is real & true & very rarely what you expect.

In my work as an artist, most of the time I don't have the faintest idea what's going to happen. I sit down & feel the world around me & in me. I become enchanted, in the best sense of the word - I am filled with delight. I listen to the voices of my heart. I draw a line. I draw another line. I remember the time I won a whole bag of marbles from my next-door neighbor. I remember going to the beach with all my cousins. I draw more lines. I remember more things. I keep putting down lines. Every line is a whisper of memory, of my life at that moment. People ask me how I come up with the stuff I do. I tell them it's all right there when I listen. It is a powerful act of love to simply listen well & fully.

At some point while I was playing with the pieces of this fifth book, it struck me that perhaps these stories were the Philosopher's Stones. Our stories make the dead dance & the living soar. They turn water into wine & rocks into gold. They give us power beyond our wildest dreams. Perhaps our stories do something even greater than that, something we haven't even considered in our small vision. Something like helping us all to listen. Reminding us to pay attention to the soft voices. Perhaps. There may be answers hidden in the quick connections of this book. Or maybe they're just beyond the edges, waiting for us to hear. Until then, I've enjoyed putting these stories together. I hope you will, too...

With love,

Brian Andreas
Bastille Day, 14 July 1998

I used to hear
voices a lot,
but then I read
up on it &
found out
they don't exist

so now I don't
listen to a word
they say.

Hearing Voices

One morning she decided to throw away the paper & not say a word & listen to the real news & by the end of the day, she knew that while people were sometimes confused, the rest of the world was not & she slept soundly that night for the first time since she was a young girl.

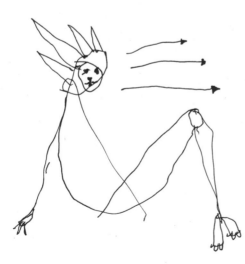

Just because I keep my eyes open doesn't mean I'm paying attention Sometimes I'm just trying to get my contacts to slide back in place.

The most important
thing

stuff that'll
be worth
something
someday
when
people's
priorities
change

you leave behind

is the stuff that

turns into

treasures

when children

find it

Treasures

It's hard to say
the right words
without practice,
I said & she
whispered in my
ear, Say them
as many times
as you like

& we practiced
late into the
night

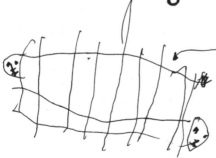

tied together by stuff
too difficult
to explain to
someone new

Right Practice

How'd it go at soccer?
I said & he said we worked
on fundamentals & I said
like why you were even
chasing around after a
ball in the first place?

    & from the way he
    looked at me I
    figured out that
    was probably
    too fundamental.

There's a lot of space
in here I'm just
starting to discover,
my grandma told me
not long ago, so
I'm hoping my body
holds out.

this is where I keep
things I agreed to do
before I found out how
difficult they would be

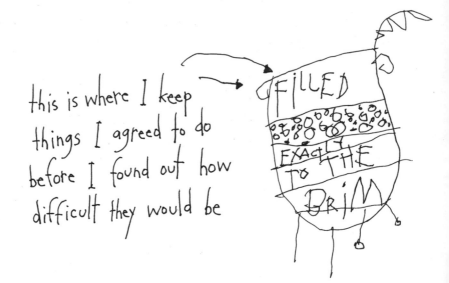

Just because they die, she said,
doesn't mean they
go away

Permanence

It's hardest to
love the ordinary
things, she said,
but you get lots
of opportunities
to practice.

scattering little bits of happiness
everywhere she goes, except
at home because her
family told her to get
out

& leave them in
peace for godsakes

We sat
side by side
in the morning
light

& looked out
at the future
together .

Side by Side

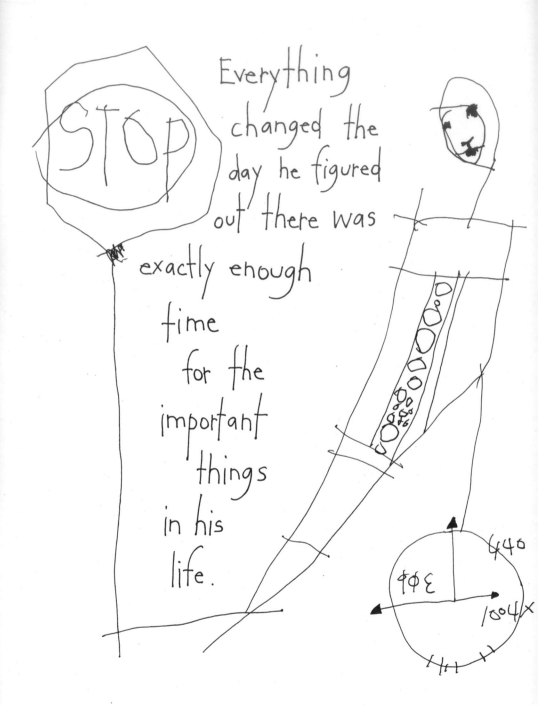

Everything changed the day he figured out there was exactly enough time for the important things in his life.

Enough Time

I would not
say I love
you so much
if you could
teach me
a better way,
I said
& she said
that'd do fine
for now.

melting in
the
slow

heat of
a summer
night. damp with the
dark air   & thoughts of you

After all those years,
she was nothing like
I remembered, but
my heart leaped
across the gap anyway
without a moment's
hesitation .

standing in the twilight watching the world with soft dark eyes

Without Hesitation

What do I get for
this? I said & the
angel gave me a
catalog filled with
toasters & clock radios
& a basketball signed
by Michael Jordan &
I said, But this is
just stuff & the angel
smiled & swallowed
me in her arms.
    I'm so glad you
    said that, she
    whispered to me.
        I knew you still
        had a chance.

Fighting Chance

I've been having the
hardest time today
coming up with
excuses, she said.

I think I'm
having a
work ethic
flashback.

I don't want another opportunity to learn
& grow, she said. I just want to eat
crackers & watch Oprah & pet my cat.

Two can live as cheaply as one
if one of us didn't like
chocolate so much

Ever since I found
out I was schizophrenic,
he said, I've been
making up songs
that are easy to
harmonize with.

I really like a
good sing-a-long.

Sing Along

Do you ever listen to me?, she said & I said I did,

but sometimes it took a couple of days to sort it out in a way that didn't make me want to murder, her, in her, sleep.

this is a box filled with all the time in the world & most people are amazed it fits in such a small space

Tolerance

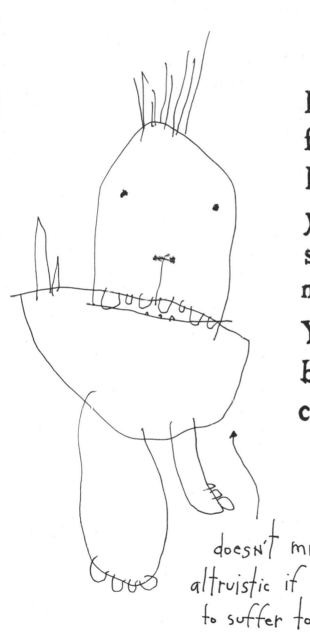

It's only
fair when
I yell at
you, she
said to
me once.
You had a
better
childhood.

doesn't mind being
altruistic if he doesn't have
to suffer to do it

Better Childhood

connected by
a silver cord
that hums
with sadness
the further
it is stretched

I always imagine
the worst possible
thing that can
happen, she told
me. It gives me a
great excuse to stay
home & have tea.

Worst Case

I don't want anything
from you, I said,
unless you want me
to want something
from you

      & she smiled
& said, I knew you
were in one of those
moods

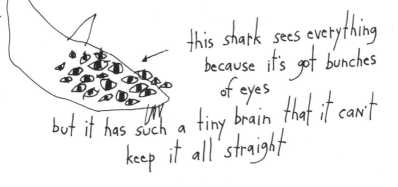

this shark sees everything
because it's got bunches
of eyes
but it has such a tiny brain that it can't
keep it all straight

The only reason my cat's still with me, she said, is that he hides quicker than everybody else.

How do you know if
God's on your side?
he said & I said,
if you live long enough to
write it down.
At least. that's the way it
seems to work.

Of course I act
like a barbarian,
he said. They're
the only ones who
have any fun in
this life.

standing by
the window
watching his
father go
off to run
the world

I'll bet you do something important, he said

& I said the most important thing

was watching while he slept

& he
said he'd
do the same
for me someday
& we shook hands   & decided it was a
                        fair trade.

Fair Trade

Why do you tell the truth?
my son asked & I thought
about it for awhile & finally
I said, Because human beings
get mixed up easier than
dogs & plants & fishes.
What if you're someone
who doesn't get mixed up?
he said. Go ahead & lie,
I said & then I hit him with
a pillow just because I knew
he was thinking about doing
that anyway.

You keep making

noises like that,

she told him,

& pretty soon people
will stop talking to you

& after awhile
all the kids were
over there trying
to learn how to
do it, too.

this is a cactus that thinks
there's enough violence in the
world already so it's
taking correspondence
courses in being a
cabbage

I wouldn't mind
being grownup,
she told me, if I
didn't have to
get up & be

grumpy

right away every
morning.

I used to think travelling to
exotic places would be
fun. but I have a
little more experience now
& it's only fun if it
doesn't wreck your sleep.

Morning Person

I sometimes wake in the early morning
& listen to the soft breathing
of my children

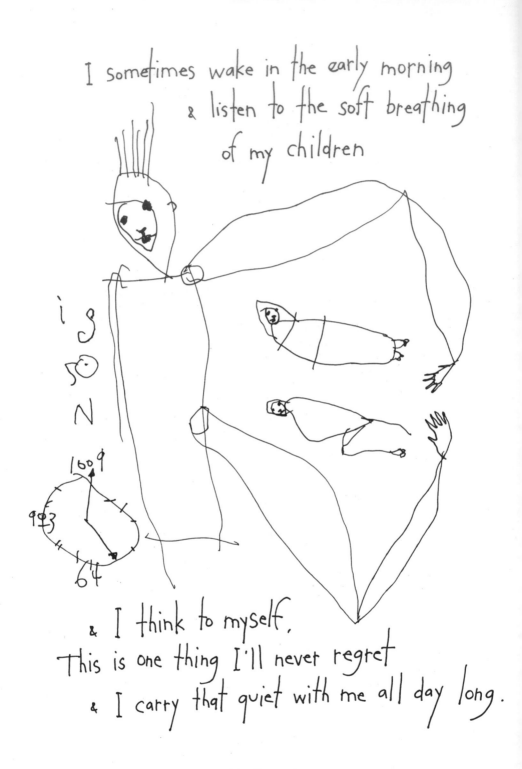

& I think to myself,
This is one thing I'll never regret
& I carry that quiet with me all day long.

No Regret

I don't read the paper
& I don't watch tv &
people ask me how I
stay up with what's
going on & I tell them
breathing seems to
help & since I haven't
done serious damage
to anyone yet, they
usually leave me alone.

filled to the brim with
dangerous thoughts &
nowhere to put them
since she lives in a small town
& everybody's always watching

I think we should
make all the flags
in the parade out
of long underwear,
he said, because
then only the really
fun people will
come.

You can't just say stuff like that,
she told me. people will think you're
serious & I nodded
& said I know & won't they

be surprised
when they finally figure it out &
she shook her head & said she should
probably make plans then for a backup husband.

Underwear Parade

You're the strangest person
I ever met, she said
& I said
You too
& we
decided we'd
know each
other
a long time

Kindred Spirit

I finally settled
on Buddhism,
she said, but it's
more than just a
fashion statement.
I've always done
some of my best
work in my bathrobe.

You look like someone from the 70's,
I said & she smiled & said that
this time around she'd done it
by choice & that made it easier

Yellow Bathrobe

fake leopard that she cut out
of a coat she got
from the
Salvation Army

Polyester
expedition
led By an
experienced
guide

You don't see stuff like
this every day, she said
& I said some things
go extinct for very good
reasons & she snorted
& said I didn't know
much about fashion, did I?

Extinct

I don't care if no one likes it, she said,

unless
no one
likes it.

has detached with love
so many times that her
hair has started to
fall out in clumps

Apathy

I'm the last person you should ask about weird, he told me, I was raised in the suburbs of America

If you get a tight enough perm, she told me, it's almost as good as a face lift.

But she had worked around a lot of toxic chemicals in the 60's, so I gave her the benefit of the doubt.

Tight Perm

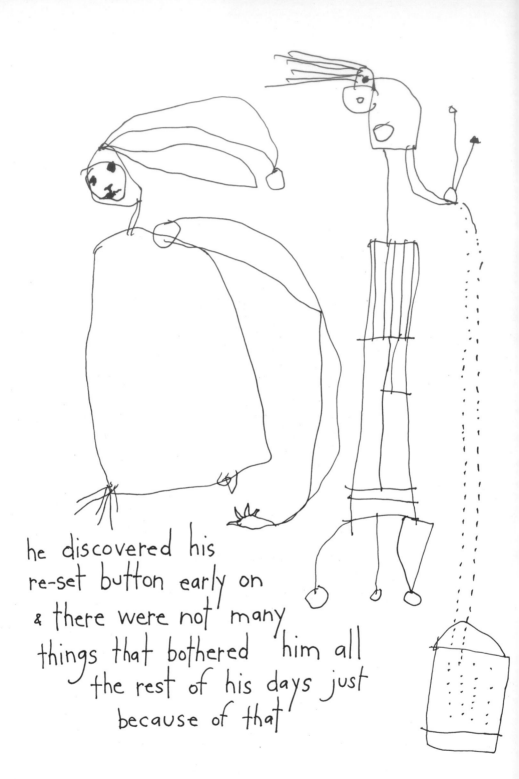

he discovered his
re-set button early on
& there were not many
things that bothered him all
the rest of his days just
because of that

Reset Button

If you can't laugh at yourself, my grandpa told me, you're not doing enough stupid things. I told him I didn't usually run out of stupid things, but it's hard to laugh that long at anything.

100000000 VolTS

Do not put your tongue or your finger or any body parts in here no matter how fun you think it would be because it wouldn't

Stupid Things

I've learned not to
look too closely,
she said. Otherwise
I'd just keep finding
out stuff that'd bug
me & we'd never
get along.

← these guys
are mainly
scarey because
they don't
exfoliate
& it hides their inner beauty

My mother always told me to finish what I started, but she had no idea of some of the people I'd be dealing with

SOMEPLACE with less PEODLE i KNOW

A to Z

I always wanted to invent something that would move around & make funny noises & would change the world as we know it

& I forgot all about that until we had kids & now I see I came pretty close.

Hop Hop

Invention

What would it take to
fly? he said & I said
I wasn't sure, but I
knew he'd have to
move faster than he
did now & he thought
about that for a
minute & then he looked
at me & said you're
trying to teach me
something, aren't you?

We stood out on the porch before we went inside & she told me her secret.

Pretend you're just visiting, she said. That way you'll forget that they're family.

wishes only for things she can't have because it is a perfect excuse for never getting anything done

If you kill your brother, she said, you're going to get a huge timeout.

100 YEARS

WITH TIME OFF FOR GOOD BEHAVIOR

I would like to think
more about baseball
& small engines &
the best weedkiller
known to man, but
I always end up
watching the ants on
my back porch,
thinking we're not
so different after all.

CERTIFIED
MISSING LINK

given a choice between
science & religion I'd
probably stick with
science, but I still
wouldn't trust it to figure out
anything important either.

Watching Ants

washing along with all the rest
of the people in the mall
trying to burn off all the calories
from the food park

I like butter
& sugar & being alive
a whole lot

& today I'm
kind of sad because
with all the latest
studies
I figured out
I'm going to have
to choose.

Butter & Sugar

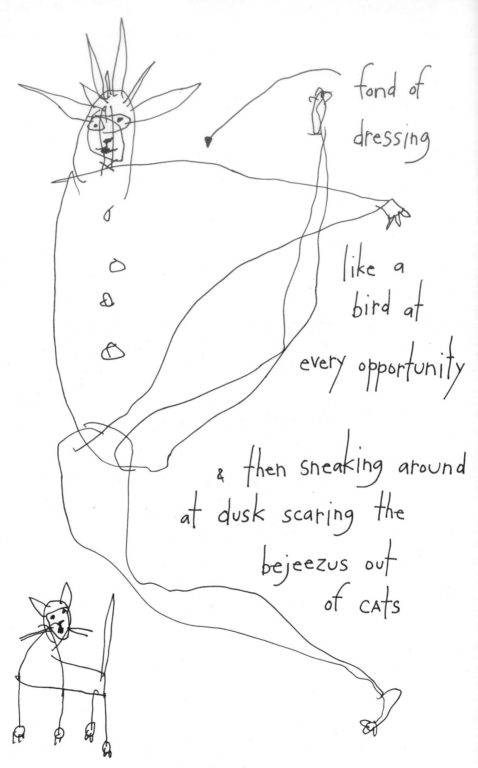

fond of
dressing

like a
bird at

every opportunity

& then sneaking around
at dusk scaring the
bejeezus out
of cats

Bird Costume

just happy knowing it might have been
possible in another life & that
moment brought him joy
many times after that

We sat in the car
& the night dropped
down until the
only sounds were
the crickets &
the dance of our
voices

& for a moment
the world became
small enough to
roll back & forth
between us

Small World

You'll have to tell me over the phone, she said. I checked with my mirror & it told me I was too scary to go out today.

she heard from her only when things were going poorly. We have more to talk about when I can give her advice, she said.

Scary Mirror

I'm too lazy to
get enlightened,
he told
me once

& I like restaurants
too much.

What does that have
to do with anything? I said.

I'm not sure, he said,
but any excuse is good
when there's
change involved.

Good Excuse

I wish I knew
what this means
but I wish that
about a lot of
things so mostly
I enjoy not
knowing

I've never been
that good at
complaining,
she told me,
because I'm
going to be
dead in another
50 years & it's
all going to
change then
anyway.

Basically excited about life
as long as he doesn't
look too closely at how
much he has to do

Perpetual Change

When I told him
I had a major in
English, he said
too bad for you
this is **America**
then & he started
me out at the
bottom.

LIVE NUDE
MUD wrestling
to Big
Band &
Country
crossover

You couldn't get away
with half this stuff
where I live, he
said. Nobody'd
get anything done.

English Major

I saw Jacques Cousteau
at the grocery store in L.A.
once & I watched to see
what he would buy,

but he only got corn
chips & some shoelaces

& I don't know what
I expected, but I
would've settled for
a can of chunk light

tuna even.

If /\ I'd been more enlightened I don't think I'd have
come back as an American, she told me, but
think of all the great videos I would've missed.

Jacques Cousteau

he wanted to be big
so he could do
all the fun stuff

but small was
better when it
came to getting
out of work

Pragmatic

I've had cats
since I was
young, she
said & I still
love them.
See, I said,
you don't
have to be
smart to be
happy.

he's always stretched out on
the couch

on a steady diet of chee·tohs
& raspberries

& his usual excuse is, It must have been something I ate.

Cat Lover

Some of the stuff
I learned early on
was useful, she told
me, but most of it
was obviously meant
for someone who was
not me.

Weight

I had a teacher once who said the greatest mystery of the universe was her husband & after that I could never understand why we wasted so much time on things like the cure for cancer or putting a man on the moon when we could just have all those scientists working on him.

Mystery of the Universe

I could never
live in

Paradise,

she said .

I don't look
that good
naked .

thinks about moving to
someplace else where
everything is different
enough to be fun
again

they drove south one winter until they could stand outside with no coats on

& we never saw them again

Heading South

I have a friend who does
numerology in California
& she called me up one
night & said that 444
was the number of
Wal-Mart, which is
30 percent off of 666
& we were both amazed

   & then I hung up the
   phone & said now I
   remember why we
   moved to Iowa.

Time to come out, I told him
& he said he'd only been in
for 6 minutes & I said that's
not true. You've been in the
whole day & he shrugged &
said all he could remember
was the last 6 minutes.

If I'm asleep. he said, how will I know if I
miss anything?

& I promised I'd
leave him a note.

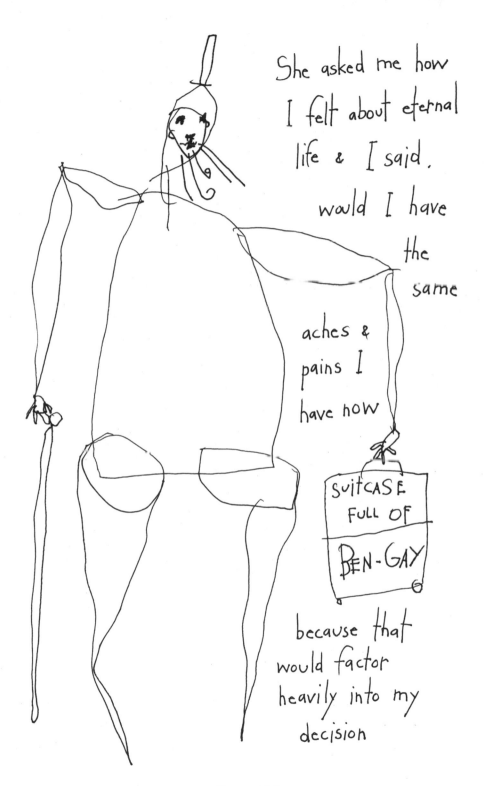

She asked me how I felt about eternal life & I said, would I have the same aches & pains I have now

SUITCASE FULL OF BEN-GAY

because that would factor heavily into my decision

Eternal Life

Some days
I wonder how
my kids will
turn out,
but most
of the time
I'm just
figuring out
how to survive them
right now.

Survival

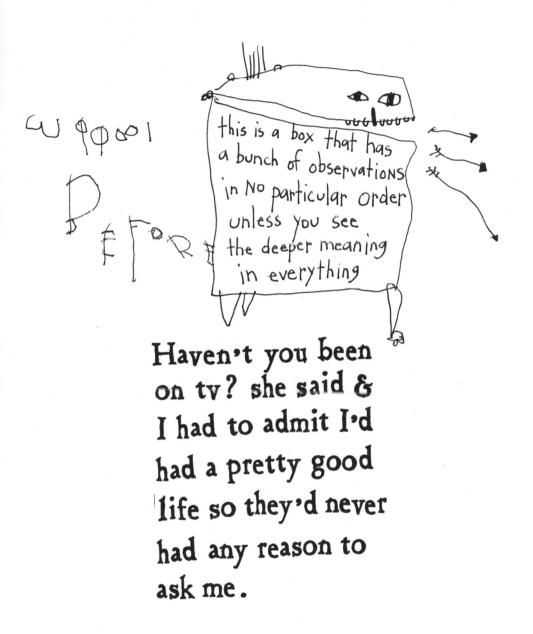

this is a box that has a bunch of observations in no particular order unless you see the deeper meaning in everything

Haven't you been on tv? she said & I had to admit I'd had a pretty good life so they'd never had any reason to ask me.

I like people until
they give me reason
not to, she said.

Some days they
just drop like flies,
though, she added.

Dropping Like Flies

I still fly a lot in my dreams, she told us, but I try to stay close to the ground. At my age a fall can be pretty serious.

Can you prove any of the
stuff you believe in?
my son asked me & when
I said that's not how
belief works, he nodded
& said that's what he
thought but he was just
checking to make sure
he hadn't missed a key
point.

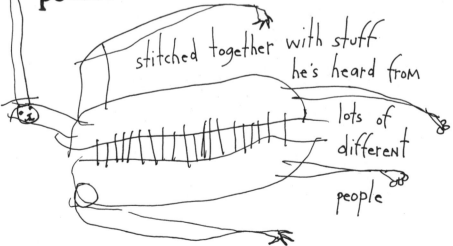

stitched together with stuff
he's heard from
lots of
different
people

I don't mind waiting
for a little while, he
said, if I get a treat
in the end.

What do you think
is a treat? I said.

Not having to

wait

too long, he said

& I had to give him
points for honesty.

Wish for your deepest desires,
she said
& when I asked if
they'd come true, she
said they always
do,

BED OF NAILS THAT YOU GET
USED TO AFTER A WHILE

so you might as well get
them out in the open while
you're still young enough
to correct any serious mistakes.

Deepest Desires

In the end,
I think I will
like that we were
sitting on the bed,
talking
& wondering where
the time had gone.

About the Artist

Brian Andreas is a fiber artist, sculptor, and storyteller. He uses traditional media from fine art, theatre and storytelling, as well as electronic media to explore new forms of human community. He also likes to put things together with the rustiest stuff he can find. His work is shown and collected internationally.

Born in 1956 in Iowa City, Iowa, he holds a B.A. from Luther College in Decorah, Iowa, and an M.F.A. in Fiber and Mixed Media from John F. Kennedy University in Orinda, California.

After years of adventure on the West Coast of the United States, he now lives together with his wife, Ellen, and their two children in Iowa, where he writes most of his new stories on little white restaurant napkins, and reminisces about great meals he's had in other places.

About StoryPeople

StoryPeople are wood sculptures, three to four feet tall, in a roughly human form. They can be as varied as a simple cutout figure, or an assemblage of found and scrap wood, or an intricate, roughly made treasure box. Each piece uses only recycled barn and fence wood from old homesteads in the northeast Iowa area. Adding to their individual quirkiness are scraps of old barn tin and twists of wire. They are painted with bright colors and hand-stamped, a letter at a time, with original stories. The most striking aspect of StoryPeople are the shaded spirit faces. These faces are softly blended into the wood surface, and make each StoryPerson come alive.

Every figure is signed and numbered, and is unique because of the materials used. The figures, the colorful story prints, and the books, are available in galleries and stores throughout the US, Canada & the UK. Please feel free to call or write for more information, or drop in at our web site.

StoryPeople
P.O. Box 7
Decorah, IA 52101
USA

800.476.7178
319.382.8060
319.382.0263 FAX

orders@storypeople.com
http://www.storypeople.com